2022

SWIMMING PLANNER

THIS BELONGS TO

PHONE NUMBER

ABOUT THIS BOOK

Whether you swim for fun, fitness, or competition, keeping track of your swims is a great way to measure improvement and continually motivate yourself.

This Swimming planner contains everything needed for a Swimner, from beginner to professional and for everyone in between. We understand that each individual will have different needs, so feel free to use this book how best suits you. You may decide to leave some section blank (E.g. heart rate and calories if fitness is not your goal), and there are plenty of lined notes pages at the back of the book should you require space for something not tracked in this book.

A list of items included of this book includes:

- **2022 Year at a glance calendar** with space for noting down important dates for the year
- **2022 Monthly calendar** (2 Page spread)
- **Weekly / daily calendar** with space each day for notes about your swim, as well inputs for Distance, Time, Pace, Heart rate and Calories burned.
- **Total distance tracker** to add up distance swam over the year
- **Goals checklist** - What are your personal goals for the year?
- **Goal race list** - Which races would you like to attend this year? Includes location and date
- **Race results** - Track your pace, distance, time and placement for each race you compete in
- **Yearly reflection** - Space for you to reflect on the year with suggestions on topics to write about.
- **Lined notes pages** with date, for you to use how best fits your needs.

We suggest having a good look through the book before using it, to ensure you know which elements of your Swimming journey to keep note of! On the next page is a sample of **some** of the pages contained in this book.

2022 CALENDAR

January / February / March / April / May / June

IMPORTANT DATES

DATE	DESCRIPTION

YEARLY RECAP

Total Distance Swum	
Longest Swim	
Number of Swims	
Number of Races Swum	
Total Distance (Race)	
Quickest Pace (Race)	
Best Placement in a Race	
Average Race Placement	
Longest Weekly Distance	
Longest Monthly Distance	

JANUARY

MONDAY	TUESDAY	WEDNESDAY	THURSDAY	FRIDAY	SATURDAY	SUNDAY	NOTES
27	28	29	30	31	1	2	
3	4	5	6	7	8	9	
10	11	12	13	14	15	16	
17	18	19	20	21	22	23	
24	25	26	27	28	29	30	
31	1	2	3	4	5	6	

MY RACE RESULTS

DATE	DISTANCE	TIME	PACE	PLACE

December 27, 2021 >> January 2, 2022 — Week 1

January 3, 2022 >> January 9, 2022 — Week 2

NOTES

DATE	NOTE

January

M	T	W	T	F	S	S
					1	2
3	4	5	6	7	8	9
10	11	12	13	14	15	16
17	18	19	20	21	22	23
24	25	26	27	28	29	30
31						

February

M	T	W	T	F	S	S
	1	2	3	4	5	6
7	8	9	10	11	12	13
14	15	16	17	18	19	20
21	22	23	24	25	26	27
28						

March

M	T	W	T	F	S	S
	1	2	3	4	5	6
7	8	9	10	11	12	13
14	15	16	17	18	19	20
21	22	23	24	25	26	27
28	29	30	31			

April

M	T	W	T	F	S	S
				1	2	3
4	5	6	7	8	9	10
11	12	13	14	15	16	17
18	19	20	21	22	23	24
25	26	27	28	29	30	

May

M	T	W	T	F	S	S
						1
2	3	4	5	6	7	8
9	10	11	12	13	14	15
16	17	18	19	20	21	22
23	24	25	26	27	28	29
30	31					

June

M	T	W	T	F	S	S
		1	2	3	4	5
6	7	8	9	10	11	12
13	14	15	16	17	18	19
20	21	22	23	24	25	26
27	28	29	30			

DATE	DESCRIPTION

July

M	T	W	T	F	S	S
				1	2	3
4	5	6	7	8	9	10
11	12	13	14	15	16	17
18	19	20	21	22	23	24
25	26	27	28	29	30	31

August

M	T	W	T	F	S	S
1	2	3	4	5	6	7
8	9	10	11	12	13	14
15	16	17	18	19	20	21
22	23	24	25	26	27	28
29	30	31				

September

M	T	W	T	F	S	S
			1	2	3	4
5	6	7	8	9	10	11
12	13	14	15	16	17	18
19	20	21	22	23	24	25
26	27	28	29	30		

October

M	T	W	T	F	S	S
					1	2
3	4	5	6	7	8	9
10	11	12	13	14	15	16
17	18	19	20	21	22	23
24	25	26	27	28	29	30
31						

November

M	T	W	T	F	S	S
	1	2	3	4	5	6
7	8	9	10	11	12	13
14	15	16	17	18	19	20
21	22	23	24	25	26	27
28	29	30	1	2	3	4

December

M	T	W	T	F	S	S
			1	2	3	4
5	6	7	8	9	10	11
12	13	14	15	16	17	18
19	20	21	22	23	24	25
26	27	28	29	30	31	

DATE	DESCRIPTION

GOALS

GOAL	X	DATE ACHIEVED

GOAL	X	DATE ACHIEVED

GOAL RACE LIST

DATE	RACE	RACE LOCATION	X

DATE	RACE	RACE LOCATION	X

MY RACE RESULTS

DATE	DISTANCE	TIME	PACE	PLACE

MY RACE RESULTS

DATE	DISTANCE	TIME	PACE	PLACE

MONDAY	TUESDAY	WEDNESDAY	THURSDAY
27	28	29	30
3	4	5	6
10	11	12	13
17	18	19	20
24	25	26	27
31	1	2	3

FRIDAY	SATURDAY	SUNDAY	NOTES
31	1	2	
7	8	9	
14	15	16	
21	22	23	
28	29	30	
4	5	6	

FEBRUARY

MONDAY	TUESDAY	WEDNESDAY	THURSDAY
31	1	2	3
7	8	9	10
14	15	16	17
21	22	23	24
28	1	2	3

FRIDAY	SATURDAY	SUNDAY	NOTES
4	5	6	
11	12	13	
18	19	20	
25	26	27	
4	5	6	

MONDAY	TUESDAY	WEDNESDAY	THURSDAY
28	1	2	3
7	8	9	10
14	15	16	17
21	22	23	24
28	29	30	31

FRIDAY	SATURDAY	SUNDAY	NOTES
4	5	6	
11	12	13	
18	19	20	
25	26	27	
1	2	3	

APRIL

MONDAY	TUESDAY	WEDNESDAY	THURSDAY
28	29	30	31
4	5	6	7
11	12	13	14
18	19	20	21
25	26	27	28

FRIDAY	SATURDAY	SUNDAY	NOTES
1	2	3	
8	9	10	
15	16	17	
22	23	24	
29	30	1	

MONDAY	TUESDAY	WEDNESDAY	THURSDAY
25	26	27	28
2	3	4	5
9	10	11	12
16	17	18	19
23	24	25	26
30	31	1	2

FRIDAY	SATURDAY	SUNDAY	NOTES
29	30	1	
6	7	8	
13	14	15	
20	21	22	
27	28	29	
3	4	5	

MONDAY	TUESDAY	WEDNESDAY	THURSDAY
30	31	1	2
6	7	8	9
13	14	15	16
20	21	22	23
27	28	29	30

FRIDAY	SATURDAY	SUNDAY	NOTES
3	4	5	
10	11	12	
17	18	19	
24	25	26	
1	2	3	

MONDAY	TUESDAY	WEDNESDAY	THURSDAY
27	28	29	30
4	5	6	7
11	12	13	14
18	19	20	21
25	26	27	28

FRIDAY	SATURDAY	SUNDAY	NOTES
1	2	3	
8	9	10	
15	16	17	
22	23	24	
29	30	31	

MONDAY	TUESDAY	WEDNESDAY	THURSDAY
1	2	3	4
8	9	10	11
15	16	17	18
22	23	24	25
29	30	31	1

FRIDAY	SATURDAY	SUNDAY	NOTES
5	6	7	
12	13	14	
19	20	21	
26	27	28	
2	3	4	

SEPTEMBER

MONDAY	TUESDAY	WEDNESDAY	THURSDAY
29	30	31	1
5	6	7	8
12	13	14	15
19	20	21	22
26	27	28	29

FRIDAY	SATURDAY	SUNDAY	NOTES
2	3	4	
9	10	11	
16	17	18	
23	24	25	
30	1	2	

OCTOBER

MONDAY	TUESDAY	WEDNESDAY	THURSDAY
26	27	28	29
3	4	5	6
10	11	12	13
17	18	19	20
24	25	26	27
31	1	2	3

FRIDAY	SATURDAY	SUNDAY	NOTES
30	1	2	
7	8	9	
14	15	16	
21	22	23	
28	29	30	
4	5	6	

MONDAY	TUESDAY	WEDNESDAY	THURSDAY
31	1	2	3
7	8	9	10
14	15	16	17
21	22	23	24
28	29	30	1

FRIDAY	SATURDAY	SUNDAY	NOTES
4	5	6	
11	12	13	
18	19	20	
25	26	27	
2	3	4	

DECEMBER

MONDAY	TUESDAY	WEDNESDAY	THURSDAY
28	29	30	1
5	6	7	8
12	13	14	15
19	20	21	22
26	27	28	29

FRIDAY	SATURDAY	SUNDAY	NOTES
2	3	4	
9	10	11	
16	17	18	
23	24	25	
30	31	1	

Monday **27** December	☐ Ocean ☐ Pool Laps _____ Pool Length _____		DISTANCE	
			TIME	
			PACE	
			HEART RATE	
			CALORIES	
Tuesday **28** December	☐ Ocean ☐ Pool Laps _____ Pool Length _____		DISTANCE	
			TIME	
			PACE	
			HEART RATE	
			CALORIES	
Wednesday **29** December	☐ Ocean ☐ Pool Laps _____ Pool Length _____		DISTANCE	
			TIME	
			PACE	
			HEART RATE	
			CALORIES	
Thursday **30** December	☐ Ocean ☐ Pool Laps _____ Pool Length _____		DISTANCE	
			TIME	
			PACE	
			HEART RATE	
			CALORIES	
Friday **31** December	☐ Ocean ☐ Pool Laps _____ Pool Length _____		DISTANCE	
			TIME	
			PACE	
			HEART RATE	
			CALORIES	
Saturday **1** January	☐ Ocean ☐ Pool Laps _____ Pool Length _____		DISTANCE	
			TIME	
			PACE	
			HEART RATE	
			CALORIES	
Sunday **2** January	☐ Ocean ☐ Pool Laps _____ Pool Length _____		DISTANCE	
			TIME	
			PACE	
			HEART RATE	
			CALORIES	

NOTES, ACHIEVEMENTS, EXTRA TRAINING

THIS WEEKS DISTANCE	
TOTAL YEARLY DISTANCE	

Monday **3** January	☐ Ocean ☐ Pool Laps _____ Pool Length _____		DISTANCE	
			TIME	
			PACE	
			HEART RATE	
			CALORIES	

Tuesday **4** January	☐ Ocean ☐ Pool Laps _____ Pool Length _____		DISTANCE	
			TIME	
			PACE	
			HEART RATE	
			CALORIES	

Wednesday **5** January	☐ Ocean ☐ Pool Laps _____ Pool Length _____		DISTANCE	
			TIME	
			PACE	
			HEART RATE	
			CALORIES	

Thursday **6** January	☐ Ocean ☐ Pool Laps _____ Pool Length _____		DISTANCE	
			TIME	
			PACE	
			HEART RATE	
			CALORIES	

Friday **7** January	☐ Ocean ☐ Pool Laps _____ Pool Length _____		DISTANCE	
			TIME	
			PACE	
			HEART RATE	
			CALORIES	

Saturday **8** January	☐ Ocean ☐ Pool Laps _____ Pool Length _____		DISTANCE	
			TIME	
			PACE	
			HEART RATE	
			CALORIES	

Sunday **9** January	☐ Ocean ☐ Pool Laps _____ Pool Length _____		DISTANCE	
			TIME	
			PACE	
			HEART RATE	
			CALORIES	

NOTES, ACHIEVEMENTS, EXTRA TRAINING

| THIS WEEKS DISTANCE | |
| TOTAL YEARLY DISTANCE | |

Monday **10** January	☐ Ocean ☐ Pool Laps _____ Pool Length _____		DISTANCE	
			TIME	
			PACE	
			HEART RATE	
			CALORIES	
Tuesday **11** January	☐ Ocean ☐ Pool Laps _____ Pool Length _____		DISTANCE	
			TIME	
			PACE	
			HEART RATE	
			CALORIES	
Wednesday **12** January	☐ Ocean ☐ Pool Laps _____ Pool Length _____		DISTANCE	
			TIME	
			PACE	
			HEART RATE	
			CALORIES	
Thursday **13** January	☐ Ocean ☐ Pool Laps _____ Pool Length _____		DISTANCE	
			TIME	
			PACE	
			HEART RATE	
			CALORIES	
Friday **14** January	☐ Ocean ☐ Pool Laps _____ Pool Length _____		DISTANCE	
			TIME	
			PACE	
			HEART RATE	
			CALORIES	
Saturday **15** January	☐ Ocean ☐ Pool Laps _____ Pool Length _____		DISTANCE	
			TIME	
			PACE	
			HEART RATE	
			CALORIES	
Sunday **16** January	☐ Ocean ☐ Pool Laps _____ Pool Length _____		DISTANCE	
			TIME	
			PACE	
			HEART RATE	
			CALORIES	

NOTES, ACHIEVEMENTS, EXTRA TRAINING

THIS WEEKS DISTANCE	
TOTAL YEARLY DISTANCE	

Monday **17** January	☐ Ocean ☐ Pool Laps _____ Pool Length _____		DISTANCE	
			TIME	
			PACE	
			HEART RATE	
			CALORIES	
Tuesday **18** January	☐ Ocean ☐ Pool Laps _____ Pool Length _____		DISTANCE	
			TIME	
			PACE	
			HEART RATE	
			CALORIES	
Wednesday **19** January	☐ Ocean ☐ Pool Laps _____ Pool Length _____		DISTANCE	
			TIME	
			PACE	
			HEART RATE	
			CALORIES	
Thursday **20** January	☐ Ocean ☐ Pool Laps _____ Pool Length _____		DISTANCE	
			TIME	
			PACE	
			HEART RATE	
			CALORIES	
Friday **21** January	☐ Ocean ☐ Pool Laps _____ Pool Length _____		DISTANCE	
			TIME	
			PACE	
			HEART RATE	
			CALORIES	
Saturday **22** January	☐ Ocean ☐ Pool Laps _____ Pool Length _____		DISTANCE	
			TIME	
			PACE	
			HEART RATE	
			CALORIES	
Sunday **23** January	☐ Ocean ☐ Pool Laps _____ Pool Length _____		DISTANCE	
			TIME	
			PACE	
			HEART RATE	
			CALORIES	

NOTES, ACHIEVEMENTS, EXTRA TRAINING

| THIS WEEKS DISTANCE | |
| TOTAL YEARLY DISTANCE | |

Monday 24 January	☐ Ocean ☐ Pool Laps _____ Pool Length _____		DISTANCE	
			TIME	
			PACE	
			HEART RATE	
			CALORIES	
Tuesday 25 January	☐ Ocean ☐ Pool Laps _____ Pool Length _____		DISTANCE	
			TIME	
			PACE	
			HEART RATE	
			CALORIES	
Wednesday 26 January	☐ Ocean ☐ Pool Laps _____ Pool Length _____		DISTANCE	
			TIME	
			PACE	
			HEART RATE	
			CALORIES	
Thursday 27 January	☐ Ocean ☐ Pool Laps _____ Pool Length _____		DISTANCE	
			TIME	
			PACE	
			HEART RATE	
			CALORIES	
Friday 28 January	☐ Ocean ☐ Pool Laps _____ Pool Length _____		DISTANCE	
			TIME	
			PACE	
			HEART RATE	
			CALORIES	
Saturday 29 January	☐ Ocean ☐ Pool Laps _____ Pool Length _____		DISTANCE	
			TIME	
			PACE	
			HEART RATE	
			CALORIES	
Sunday 30 January	☐ Ocean ☐ Pool Laps _____ Pool Length _____		DISTANCE	
			TIME	
			PACE	
			HEART RATE	
			CALORIES	

NOTES, ACHIEVEMENTS, EXTRA TRAINING

THIS WEEKS DISTANCE	
TOTAL YEARLY DISTANCE	

Monday **31** January	☐ Ocean ☐ Pool Laps _____ Pool Length _____		DISTANCE	
			TIME	
			PACE	
			HEART RATE	
			CALORIES	
Tuesday **1** February	☐ Ocean ☐ Pool Laps _____ Pool Length _____		DISTANCE	
			TIME	
			PACE	
			HEART RATE	
			CALORIES	
Wednesday **2** February	☐ Ocean ☐ Pool Laps _____ Pool Length _____		DISTANCE	
			TIME	
			PACE	
			HEART RATE	
			CALORIES	
Thursday **3** February	☐ Ocean ☐ Pool Laps _____ Pool Length _____		DISTANCE	
			TIME	
			PACE	
			HEART RATE	
			CALORIES	
Friday **4** February	☐ Ocean ☐ Pool Laps _____ Pool Length _____		DISTANCE	
			TIME	
			PACE	
			HEART RATE	
			CALORIES	
Saturday **5** February	☐ Ocean ☐ Pool Laps _____ Pool Length _____		DISTANCE	
			TIME	
			PACE	
			HEART RATE	
			CALORIES	
Sunday **6** February	☐ Ocean ☐ Pool Laps _____ Pool Length _____		DISTANCE	
			TIME	
			PACE	
			HEART RATE	
			CALORIES	

NOTES, ACHIEVEMENTS, EXTRA TRAINING

THIS WEEKS DISTANCE	
TOTAL YEARLY DISTANCE	

Monday **7** February	☐ Ocean ☐ Pool Laps _____ Pool Length _____		DISTANCE	
			TIME	
			PACE	
			HEART RATE	
			CALORIES	
Tuesday **8** February	☐ Ocean ☐ Pool Laps _____ Pool Length _____		DISTANCE	
			TIME	
			PACE	
			HEART RATE	
			CALORIES	
Wednesday **9** February	☐ Ocean ☐ Pool Laps _____ Pool Length _____		DISTANCE	
			TIME	
			PACE	
			HEART RATE	
			CALORIES	
Thursday **10** February	☐ Ocean ☐ Pool Laps _____ Pool Length _____		DISTANCE	
			TIME	
			PACE	
			HEART RATE	
			CALORIES	
Friday **11** February	☐ Ocean ☐ Pool Laps _____ Pool Length _____		DISTANCE	
			TIME	
			PACE	
			HEART RATE	
			CALORIES	
Saturday **12** February	☐ Ocean ☐ Pool Laps _____ Pool Length _____		DISTANCE	
			TIME	
			PACE	
			HEART RATE	
			CALORIES	
Sunday **13** February	☐ Ocean ☐ Pool Laps _____ Pool Length _____		DISTANCE	
			TIME	
			PACE	
			HEART RATE	
			CALORIES	

NOTES, ACHIEVEMENTS, EXTRA TRAINING

THIS WEEKS DISTANCE	
TOTAL YEARLY DISTANCE	

Monday **14** February	☐ Ocean ☐ Pool Laps ——— Pool Length ———		DISTANCE	
			TIME	
			PACE	
			HEART RATE	
			CALORIES	
Tuesday **15** February	☐ Ocean ☐ Pool Laps ——— Pool Length ———		DISTANCE	
			TIME	
			PACE	
			HEART RATE	
			CALORIES	
Wednesday **16** February	☐ Ocean ☐ Pool Laps ——— Pool Length ———		DISTANCE	
			TIME	
			PACE	
			HEART RATE	
			CALORIES	
Thursday **17** February	☐ Ocean ☐ Pool Laps ——— Pool Length ———		DISTANCE	
			TIME	
			PACE	
			HEART RATE	
			CALORIES	
Friday **18** February	☐ Ocean ☐ Pool Laps ——— Pool Length ———		DISTANCE	
			TIME	
			PACE	
			HEART RATE	
			CALORIES	
Saturday **19** February	☐ Ocean ☐ Pool Laps ——— Pool Length ———		DISTANCE	
			TIME	
			PACE	
			HEART RATE	
			CALORIES	
Sunday **20** February	☐ Ocean ☐ Pool Laps ——— Pool Length ———		DISTANCE	
			TIME	
			PACE	
			HEART RATE	
			CALORIES	

NOTES, ACHIEVEMENTS, EXTRA TRAINING

THIS WEEKS DISTANCE	
TOTAL YEARLY DISTANCE	

Monday **21** February	☐ Ocean ☐ Pool Laps _____ Pool Length _____		DISTANCE	
			TIME	
			PACE	
			HEART RATE	
			CALORIES	
Tuesday **22** February	☐ Ocean ☐ Pool Laps _____ Pool Length _____		DISTANCE	
			TIME	
			PACE	
			HEART RATE	
			CALORIES	
Wednesday **23** February	☐ Ocean ☐ Pool Laps _____ Pool Length _____		DISTANCE	
			TIME	
			PACE	
			HEART RATE	
			CALORIES	
Thursday **24** February	☐ Ocean ☐ Pool Laps _____ Pool Length _____		DISTANCE	
			TIME	
			PACE	
			HEART RATE	
			CALORIES	
Friday **25** February	☐ Ocean ☐ Pool Laps _____ Pool Length _____		DISTANCE	
			TIME	
			PACE	
			HEART RATE	
			CALORIES	
Saturday **26** February	☐ Ocean ☐ Pool Laps _____ Pool Length _____		DISTANCE	
			TIME	
			PACE	
			HEART RATE	
			CALORIES	
Sunday **27** February	☐ Ocean ☐ Pool Laps _____ Pool Length _____		DISTANCE	
			TIME	
			PACE	
			HEART RATE	
			CALORIES	

NOTES, ACHIEVEMENTS, EXTRA TRAINING

THIS WEEKS DISTANCE	
TOTAL YEARLY DISTANCE	

Monday **28** February	☐ Ocean ☐ Pool Laps _____ Pool Length _____		DISTANCE	
			TIME	
			PACE	
			HEART RATE	
			CALORIES	
Tuesday **1** March	☐ Ocean ☐ Pool Laps _____ Pool Length _____		DISTANCE	
			TIME	
			PACE	
			HEART RATE	
			CALORIES	
Wednesday **2** March	☐ Ocean ☐ Pool Laps _____ Pool Length _____		DISTANCE	
			TIME	
			PACE	
			HEART RATE	
			CALORIES	
Thursday **3** March	☐ Ocean ☐ Pool Laps _____ Pool Length _____		DISTANCE	
			TIME	
			PACE	
			HEART RATE	
			CALORIES	
Friday **4** March	☐ Ocean ☐ Pool Laps _____ Pool Length _____		DISTANCE	
			TIME	
			PACE	
			HEART RATE	
			CALORIES	
Saturday **5** March	☐ Ocean ☐ Pool Laps _____ Pool Length _____		DISTANCE	
			TIME	
			PACE	
			HEART RATE	
			CALORIES	
Sunday **6** March	☐ Ocean ☐ Pool Laps _____ Pool Length _____		DISTANCE	
			TIME	
			PACE	
			HEART RATE	
			CALORIES	

NOTES, ACHIEVEMENTS, EXTRA TRAINING

THIS WEEKS DISTANCE	
TOTAL YEARLY DISTANCE	

			DISTANCE	
Monday **7** March	☐ Ocean ☐ Pool Laps _____ Pool Length _____		TIME	
			PACE	
			HEART RATE	
			CALORIES	
Tuesday **8** March	☐ Ocean ☐ Pool Laps _____ Pool Length _____		DISTANCE	
			TIME	
			PACE	
			HEART RATE	
			CALORIES	
Wednesday **9** March	☐ Ocean ☐ Pool Laps _____ Pool Length _____		DISTANCE	
			TIME	
			PACE	
			HEART RATE	
			CALORIES	
Thursday **10** March	☐ Ocean ☐ Pool Laps _____ Pool Length _____		DISTANCE	
			TIME	
			PACE	
			HEART RATE	
			CALORIES	
Friday **11** March	☐ Ocean ☐ Pool Laps _____ Pool Length _____		DISTANCE	
			TIME	
			PACE	
			HEART RATE	
			CALORIES	
Saturday **12** March	☐ Ocean ☐ Pool Laps _____ Pool Length _____		DISTANCE	
			TIME	
			PACE	
			HEART RATE	
			CALORIES	
Sunday **13** March	☐ Ocean ☐ Pool Laps _____ Pool Length _____		DISTANCE	
			TIME	
			PACE	
			HEART RATE	
			CALORIES	

NOTES, ACHIEVEMENTS, EXTRA TRAINING

THIS WEEKS DISTANCE	
TOTAL YEARLY DISTANCE	

Monday **14** March	☐ Ocean ☐ Pool Laps _____ Pool Length _____		DISTANCE	
			TIME	
			PACE	
			HEART RATE	
			CALORIES	
Tuesday **15** March	☐ Ocean ☐ Pool Laps _____ Pool Length _____		DISTANCE	
			TIME	
			PACE	
			HEART RATE	
			CALORIES	
Wednesday **16** March	☐ Ocean ☐ Pool Laps _____ Pool Length _____		DISTANCE	
			TIME	
			PACE	
			HEART RATE	
			CALORIES	
Thursday **17** March	☐ Ocean ☐ Pool Laps _____ Pool Length _____		DISTANCE	
			TIME	
			PACE	
			HEART RATE	
			CALORIES	
Friday **18** March	☐ Ocean ☐ Pool Laps _____ Pool Length _____		DISTANCE	
			TIME	
			PACE	
			HEART RATE	
			CALORIES	
Saturday **19** March	☐ Ocean ☐ Pool Laps _____ Pool Length _____		DISTANCE	
			TIME	
			PACE	
			HEART RATE	
			CALORIES	
Sunday **20** March	☐ Ocean ☐ Pool Laps _____ Pool Length _____		DISTANCE	
			TIME	
			PACE	
			HEART RATE	
			CALORIES	

NOTES, ACHIEVEMENTS, EXTRA TRAINING

THIS WEEKS DISTANCE	
TOTAL YEARLY DISTANCE	

			DISTANCE	
Monday ☐ Ocean ☐ Pool			TIME	
21			PACE	
	Laps _____		HEART RATE	
March	Pool Length _____		CALORIES	

			DISTANCE	
Tuesday ☐ Ocean ☐ Pool			TIME	
22			PACE	
	Laps _____		HEART RATE	
March	Pool Length _____		CALORIES	

			DISTANCE	
Wednesday ☐ Ocean ☐ Pool			TIME	
23			PACE	
	Laps _____		HEART RATE	
March	Pool Length _____		CALORIES	

			DISTANCE	
Thursday ☐ Ocean ☐ Pool			TIME	
24			PACE	
	Laps _____		HEART RATE	
March	Pool Length _____		CALORIES	

			DISTANCE	
Friday ☐ Ocean ☐ Pool			TIME	
25			PACE	
	Laps _____		HEART RATE	
March	Pool Length _____		CALORIES	

			DISTANCE	
Saturday ☐ Ocean ☐ Pool			TIME	
26			PACE	
	Laps _____		HEART RATE	
March	Pool Length _____		CALORIES	

			DISTANCE	
Sunday ☐ Ocean ☐ Pool			TIME	
27			PACE	
	Laps _____		HEART RATE	
March	Pool Length _____		CALORIES	

NOTES, ACHIEVEMENTS, EXTRA TRAINING

THIS WEEKS DISTANCE	
TOTAL YEARLY DISTANCE	

Monday **28** March	☐ Ocean ☐ Pool Laps _____ Pool Length _____		DISTANCE	
			TIME	
			PACE	
			HEART RATE	
			CALORIES	
Tuesday **29** March	☐ Ocean ☐ Pool Laps _____ Pool Length _____		DISTANCE	
			TIME	
			PACE	
			HEART RATE	
			CALORIES	
Wednesday **30** March	☐ Ocean ☐ Pool Laps _____ Pool Length _____		DISTANCE	
			TIME	
			PACE	
			HEART RATE	
			CALORIES	
Thursday **31** March	☐ Ocean ☐ Pool Laps _____ Pool Length _____		DISTANCE	
			TIME	
			PACE	
			HEART RATE	
			CALORIES	
Friday **1** April	☐ Ocean ☐ Pool Laps _____ Pool Length _____		DISTANCE	
			TIME	
			PACE	
			HEART RATE	
			CALORIES	
Saturday **2** April	☐ Ocean ☐ Pool Laps _____ Pool Length _____		DISTANCE	
			TIME	
			PACE	
			HEART RATE	
			CALORIES	
Sunday **3** April	☐ Ocean ☐ Pool Laps _____ Pool Length _____		DISTANCE	
			TIME	
			PACE	
			HEART RATE	
			CALORIES	

NOTES, ACHIEVEMENTS, EXTRA TRAINING

THIS WEEKS DISTANCE	
TOTAL YEARLY DISTANCE	

Monday **4** April	☐ Ocean ☐ Pool Laps _____ Pool Length _____		DISTANCE	
			TIME	
			PACE	
			HEART RATE	
			CALORIES	
Tuesday **5** April	☐ Ocean ☐ Pool Laps _____ Pool Length _____		DISTANCE	
			TIME	
			PACE	
			HEART RATE	
			CALORIES	
Wednesday **6** April	☐ Ocean ☐ Pool Laps _____ Pool Length _____		DISTANCE	
			TIME	
			PACE	
			HEART RATE	
			CALORIES	
Thursday **7** April	☐ Ocean ☐ Pool Laps _____ Pool Length _____		DISTANCE	
			TIME	
			PACE	
			HEART RATE	
			CALORIES	
Friday **8** April	☐ Ocean ☐ Pool Laps _____ Pool Length _____		DISTANCE	
			TIME	
			PACE	
			HEART RATE	
			CALORIES	
Saturday **9** April	☐ Ocean ☐ Pool Laps _____ Pool Length _____		DISTANCE	
			TIME	
			PACE	
			HEART RATE	
			CALORIES	
Sunday **10** April	☐ Ocean ☐ Pool Laps _____ Pool Length _____		DISTANCE	
			TIME	
			PACE	
			HEART RATE	
			CALORIES	

NOTES, ACHIEVEMENTS, EXTRA TRAINING

| THIS WEEKS DISTANCE | |
| TOTAL YEARLY DISTANCE | |

			DISTANCE	
Monday **11** April	□ Ocean □ Pool Laps _____ Pool Length _____		TIME	
			PACE	
			HEART RATE	
			CALORIES	
Tuesday **12** April	□ Ocean □ Pool Laps _____ Pool Length _____		DISTANCE	
			TIME	
			PACE	
			HEART RATE	
			CALORIES	
Wednesday **13** April	□ Ocean □ Pool Laps _____ Pool Length _____		DISTANCE	
			TIME	
			PACE	
			HEART RATE	
			CALORIES	
Thursday **14** April	□ Ocean □ Pool Laps _____ Pool Length _____		DISTANCE	
			TIME	
			PACE	
			HEART RATE	
			CALORIES	
Friday **15** April	□ Ocean □ Pool Laps _____ Pool Length _____		DISTANCE	
			TIME	
			PACE	
			HEART RATE	
			CALORIES	
Saturday **16** April	□ Ocean □ Pool Laps _____ Pool Length _____		DISTANCE	
			TIME	
			PACE	
			HEART RATE	
			CALORIES	
Sunday **17** April	□ Ocean □ Pool Laps _____ Pool Length _____		DISTANCE	
			TIME	
			PACE	
			HEART RATE	
			CALORIES	

NOTES, ACHIEVEMENTS, EXTRA TRAINING

THIS WEEKS DISTANCE	
TOTAL YEARLY DISTANCE	

Monday **18** April	☐ Ocean ☐ Pool Laps _____ Pool Length _____		DISTANCE	
			TIME	
			PACE	
			HEART RATE	
			CALORIES	
Tuesday **19** April	☐ Ocean ☐ Pool Laps _____ Pool Length _____		DISTANCE	
			TIME	
			PACE	
			HEART RATE	
			CALORIES	
Wednesday **20** April	☐ Ocean ☐ Pool Laps _____ Pool Length _____		DISTANCE	
			TIME	
			PACE	
			HEART RATE	
			CALORIES	
Thursday **21** April	☐ Ocean ☐ Pool Laps _____ Pool Length _____		DISTANCE	
			TIME	
			PACE	
			HEART RATE	
			CALORIES	
Friday **22** April	☐ Ocean ☐ Pool Laps _____ Pool Length _____		DISTANCE	
			TIME	
			PACE	
			HEART RATE	
			CALORIES	
Saturday **23** April	☐ Ocean ☐ Pool Laps _____ Pool Length _____		DISTANCE	
			TIME	
			PACE	
			HEART RATE	
			CALORIES	
Sunday **24** April	☐ Ocean ☐ Pool Laps _____ Pool Length _____		DISTANCE	
			TIME	
			PACE	
			HEART RATE	
			CALORIES	

NOTES, ACHIEVEMENTS, EXTRA TRAINING

THIS WEEKS DISTANCE	
TOTAL YEARLY DISTANCE	

Monday 25 April	☐ Ocean ☐ Pool		DISTANCE	
			TIME	
			PACE	
	Laps ———		HEART RATE	
	Pool Length ———		CALORIES	
Tuesday 26 April	☐ Ocean ☐ Pool		DISTANCE	
			TIME	
			PACE	
	Laps ———		HEART RATE	
	Pool Length ———		CALORIES	
Wednesday 27 April	☐ Ocean ☐ Pool		DISTANCE	
			TIME	
			PACE	
	Laps ———		HEART RATE	
	Pool Length ———		CALORIES	
Thursday 28 April	☐ Ocean ☐ Pool		DISTANCE	
			TIME	
			PACE	
	Laps ———		HEART RATE	
	Pool Length ———		CALORIES	
Friday 29 April	☐ Ocean ☐ Pool		DISTANCE	
			TIME	
			PACE	
	Laps ———		HEART RATE	
	Pool Length ———		CALORIES	
Saturday 30 April	☐ Ocean ☐ Pool		DISTANCE	
			TIME	
			PACE	
	Laps ———		HEART RATE	
	Pool Length ———		CALORIES	
Sunday 1 May	☐ Ocean ☐ Pool		DISTANCE	
			TIME	
			PACE	
	Laps ———		HEART RATE	
	Pool Length ———		CALORIES	

NOTES, ACHIEVEMENTS, EXTRA TRAINING

THIS WEEKS DISTANCE	
TOTAL YEARLY DISTANCE	

Monday 2 May	☐ Ocean ☐ Pool Laps ———— Pool Length ————		DISTANCE	
			TIME	
			PACE	
			HEART RATE	
			CALORIES	

Tuesday 3 May	☐ Ocean ☐ Pool Laps ———— Pool Length ————		DISTANCE	
			TIME	
			PACE	
			HEART RATE	
			CALORIES	

Wednesday 4 May	☐ Ocean ☐ Pool Laps ———— Pool Length ————		DISTANCE	
			TIME	
			PACE	
			HEART RATE	
			CALORIES	

Thursday 5 May	☐ Ocean ☐ Pool Laps ———— Pool Length ————		DISTANCE	
			TIME	
			PACE	
			HEART RATE	
			CALORIES	

Friday 6 May	☐ Ocean ☐ Pool Laps ———— Pool Length ————		DISTANCE	
			TIME	
			PACE	
			HEART RATE	
			CALORIES	

Saturday 7 May	☐ Ocean ☐ Pool Laps ———— Pool Length ————		DISTANCE	
			TIME	
			PACE	
			HEART RATE	
			CALORIES	

Sunday 8 May	☐ Ocean ☐ Pool Laps ———— Pool Length ————		DISTANCE	
			TIME	
			PACE	
			HEART RATE	
			CALORIES	

NOTES, ACHIEVEMENTS, EXTRA TRAINING

THIS WEEKS DISTANCE	
TOTAL YEARLY DISTANCE	

Monday 9 May	☐ Ocean ☐ Pool Laps _____ Pool Length _____		DISTANCE	
			TIME	
			PACE	
			HEART RATE	
			CALORIES	
Tuesday 10 May	☐ Ocean ☐ Pool Laps _____ Pool Length _____		DISTANCE	
			TIME	
			PACE	
			HEART RATE	
			CALORIES	
Wednesday 11 May	☐ Ocean ☐ Pool Laps _____ Pool Length _____		DISTANCE	
			TIME	
			PACE	
			HEART RATE	
			CALORIES	
Thursday 12 May	☐ Ocean ☐ Pool Laps _____ Pool Length _____		DISTANCE	
			TIME	
			PACE	
			HEART RATE	
			CALORIES	
Friday 13 May	☐ Ocean ☐ Pool Laps _____ Pool Length _____		DISTANCE	
			TIME	
			PACE	
			HEART RATE	
			CALORIES	
Saturday 14 May	☐ Ocean ☐ Pool Laps _____ Pool Length _____		DISTANCE	
			TIME	
			PACE	
			HEART RATE	
			CALORIES	
Sunday 15 May	☐ Ocean ☐ Pool Laps _____ Pool Length _____		DISTANCE	
			TIME	
			PACE	
			HEART RATE	
			CALORIES	

NOTES, ACHIEVEMENTS, EXTRA TRAINING

THIS WEEKS DISTANCE	
TOTAL YEARLY DISTANCE	

Monday **16** May	☐ Ocean ☐ Pool Laps _____ Pool Length _____		DISTANCE	
			TIME	
			PACE	
			HEART RATE	
			CALORIES	
Tuesday **17** May	☐ Ocean ☐ Pool Laps _____ Pool Length _____		DISTANCE	
			TIME	
			PACE	
			HEART RATE	
			CALORIES	
Wednesday **18** May	☐ Ocean ☐ Pool Laps _____ Pool Length _____		DISTANCE	
			TIME	
			PACE	
			HEART RATE	
			CALORIES	
Thursday **19** May	☐ Ocean ☐ Pool Laps _____ Pool Length _____		DISTANCE	
			TIME	
			PACE	
			HEART RATE	
			CALORIES	
Friday **20** May	☐ Ocean ☐ Pool Laps _____ Pool Length _____		DISTANCE	
			TIME	
			PACE	
			HEART RATE	
			CALORIES	
Saturday **21** May	☐ Ocean ☐ Pool Laps _____ Pool Length _____		DISTANCE	
			TIME	
			PACE	
			HEART RATE	
			CALORIES	
Sunday **22** May	☐ Ocean ☐ Pool Laps _____ Pool Length _____		DISTANCE	
			TIME	
			PACE	
			HEART RATE	
			CALORIES	

NOTES, ACHIEVEMENTS, EXTRA TRAINING

THIS WEEKS DISTANCE	
TOTAL YEARLY DISTANCE	

			DISTANCE	
Monday **23** May	☐ Ocean ☐ Pool Laps _____ Pool Length _____		TIME	
			PACE	
			HEART RATE	
			CALORIES	

			DISTANCE	
Tuesday **24** May	☐ Ocean ☐ Pool Laps _____ Pool Length _____		TIME	
			PACE	
			HEART RATE	
			CALORIES	

			DISTANCE	
Wednesday **25** May	☐ Ocean ☐ Pool Laps _____ Pool Length _____		TIME	
			PACE	
			HEART RATE	
			CALORIES	

			DISTANCE	
Thursday **26** May	☐ Ocean ☐ Pool Laps _____ Pool Length _____		TIME	
			PACE	
			HEART RATE	
			CALORIES	

			DISTANCE	
Friday **27** May	☐ Ocean ☐ Pool Laps _____ Pool Length _____		TIME	
			PACE	
			HEART RATE	
			CALORIES	

			DISTANCE	
Saturday **28** May	☐ Ocean ☐ Pool Laps _____ Pool Length _____		TIME	
			PACE	
			HEART RATE	
			CALORIES	

			DISTANCE	
Sunday **29** May	☐ Ocean ☐ Pool Laps _____ Pool Length _____		TIME	
			PACE	
			HEART RATE	
			CALORIES	

NOTES, ACHIEVEMENTS, EXTRA TRAINING

THIS WEEKS DISTANCE	
TOTAL YEARLY DISTANCE	

Monday **30** May	☐ Ocean ☐ Pool Laps ——— Pool Length ———		DISTANCE	
			TIME	
			PACE	
			HEART RATE	
			CALORIES	

Tuesday **31** May	☐ Ocean ☐ Pool Laps ——— Pool Length ———		DISTANCE	
			TIME	
			PACE	
			HEART RATE	
			CALORIES	

Wednesday **1** June	☐ Ocean ☐ Pool Laps ——— Pool Length ———		DISTANCE	
			TIME	
			PACE	
			HEART RATE	
			CALORIES	

Thursday **2** June	☐ Ocean ☐ Pool Laps ——— Pool Length ———		DISTANCE	
			TIME	
			PACE	
			HEART RATE	
			CALORIES	

Friday **3** June	☐ Ocean ☐ Pool Laps ——— Pool Length ———		DISTANCE	
			TIME	
			PACE	
			HEART RATE	
			CALORIES	

Saturday **4** June	☐ Ocean ☐ Pool Laps ——— Pool Length ———		DISTANCE	
			TIME	
			PACE	
			HEART RATE	
			CALORIES	

Sunday **5** June	☐ Ocean ☐ Pool Laps ——— Pool Length ———		DISTANCE	
			TIME	
			PACE	
			HEART RATE	
			CALORIES	

NOTES, ACHIEVEMENTS, EXTRA TRAINING

| THIS WEEKS DISTANCE | |
| TOTAL YEARLY DISTANCE | |

Monday **6** June	☐ Ocean ☐ Pool Laps _____ Pool Length _____		DISTANCE	
			TIME	
			PACE	
			HEART RATE	
			CALORIES	
Tuesday **7** June	☐ Ocean ☐ Pool Laps _____ Pool Length _____		DISTANCE	
			TIME	
			PACE	
			HEART RATE	
			CALORIES	
Wednesday **8** June	☐ Ocean ☐ Pool Laps _____ Pool Length _____		DISTANCE	
			TIME	
			PACE	
			HEART RATE	
			CALORIES	
Thursday **9** June	☐ Ocean ☐ Pool Laps _____ Pool Length _____		DISTANCE	
			TIME	
			PACE	
			HEART RATE	
			CALORIES	
Friday **10** June	☐ Ocean ☐ Pool Laps _____ Pool Length _____		DISTANCE	
			TIME	
			PACE	
			HEART RATE	
			CALORIES	
Saturday **11** June	☐ Ocean ☐ Pool Laps _____ Pool Length _____		DISTANCE	
			TIME	
			PACE	
			HEART RATE	
			CALORIES	
Sunday **12** June	☐ Ocean ☐ Pool Laps _____ Pool Length _____		DISTANCE	
			TIME	
			PACE	
			HEART RATE	
			CALORIES	

NOTES, ACHIEVEMENTS, EXTRA TRAINING

THIS WEEKS DISTANCE	
TOTAL YEARLY DISTANCE	

Monday 13 June	☐ Ocean ☐ Pool Laps _____ Pool Length _____		DISTANCE	
			TIME	
			PACE	
			HEART RATE	
			CALORIES	
Tuesday 14 June	☐ Ocean ☐ Pool Laps _____ Pool Length _____		DISTANCE	
			TIME	
			PACE	
			HEART RATE	
			CALORIES	
Wednesday 15 June	☐ Ocean ☐ Pool Laps _____ Pool Length _____		DISTANCE	
			TIME	
			PACE	
			HEART RATE	
			CALORIES	
Thursday 16 June	☐ Ocean ☐ Pool Laps _____ Pool Length _____		DISTANCE	
			TIME	
			PACE	
			HEART RATE	
			CALORIES	
Friday 17 June	☐ Ocean ☐ Pool Laps _____ Pool Length _____		DISTANCE	
			TIME	
			PACE	
			HEART RATE	
			CALORIES	
Saturday 18 June	☐ Ocean ☐ Pool Laps _____ Pool Length _____		DISTANCE	
			TIME	
			PACE	
			HEART RATE	
			CALORIES	
Sunday 19 June	☐ Ocean ☐ Pool Laps _____ Pool Length _____		DISTANCE	
			TIME	
			PACE	
			HEART RATE	
			CALORIES	

NOTES, ACHIEVEMENTS, EXTRA TRAINING

THIS WEEKS DISTANCE	
TOTAL YEARLY DISTANCE	

Monday **20** June	☐ Ocean ☐ Pool Laps _____ Pool Length _____		DISTANCE	
			TIME	
			PACE	
			HEART RATE	
			CALORIES	
Tuesday **21** June	☐ Ocean ☐ Pool Laps _____ Pool Length _____		DISTANCE	
			TIME	
			PACE	
			HEART RATE	
			CALORIES	
Wednesday **22** June	☐ Ocean ☐ Pool Laps _____ Pool Length _____		DISTANCE	
			TIME	
			PACE	
			HEART RATE	
			CALORIES	
Thursday **23** June	☐ Ocean ☐ Pool Laps _____ Pool Length _____		DISTANCE	
			TIME	
			PACE	
			HEART RATE	
			CALORIES	
Friday **24** June	☐ Ocean ☐ Pool Laps _____ Pool Length _____		DISTANCE	
			TIME	
			PACE	
			HEART RATE	
			CALORIES	
Saturday **25** June	☐ Ocean ☐ Pool Laps _____ Pool Length _____		DISTANCE	
			TIME	
			PACE	
			HEART RATE	
			CALORIES	
Sunday **26** June	☐ Ocean ☐ Pool Laps _____ Pool Length _____		DISTANCE	
			TIME	
			PACE	
			HEART RATE	
			CALORIES	

NOTES, ACHIEVEMENTS, EXTRA TRAINING

THIS WEEKS DISTANCE	
TOTAL YEARLY DISTANCE	

			DISTANCE	
Monday	☐ Ocean		TIME	
27	☐ Pool		PACE	
	Laps _____		HEART RATE	
June	Pool Length _____		CALORIES	
Tuesday	☐ Ocean		DISTANCE	
28	☐ Pool		TIME	
			PACE	
	Laps _____		HEART RATE	
June	Pool Length _____		CALORIES	
Wednesday	☐ Ocean		DISTANCE	
29	☐ Pool		TIME	
			PACE	
	Laps _____		HEART RATE	
June	Pool Length _____		CALORIES	
Thursday	☐ Ocean		DISTANCE	
30	☐ Pool		TIME	
			PACE	
	Laps _____		HEART RATE	
June	Pool Length _____		CALORIES	
Friday	☐ Ocean		DISTANCE	
1	☐ Pool		TIME	
			PACE	
	Laps _____		HEART RATE	
July	Pool Length _____		CALORIES	
Saturday	☐ Ocean		DISTANCE	
2	☐ Pool		TIME	
			PACE	
	Laps _____		HEART RATE	
July	Pool Length _____		CALORIES	
Sunday	☐ Ocean		DISTANCE	
3	☐ Pool		TIME	
			PACE	
	Laps _____		HEART RATE	
July	Pool Length _____		CALORIES	

NOTES, ACHIEVEMENTS, EXTRA TRAINING

THIS WEEKS DISTANCE	
TOTAL YEARLY DISTANCE	

Monday **4** July	☐ Ocean ☐ Pool Laps _____ Pool Length _____		DISTANCE	
			TIME	
			PACE	
			HEART RATE	
			CALORIES	

Tuesday **5** July	☐ Ocean ☐ Pool Laps _____ Pool Length _____		DISTANCE	
			TIME	
			PACE	
			HEART RATE	
			CALORIES	

Wednesday **6** July	☐ Ocean ☐ Pool Laps _____ Pool Length _____		DISTANCE	
			TIME	
			PACE	
			HEART RATE	
			CALORIES	

Thursday **7** July	☐ Ocean ☐ Pool Laps _____ Pool Length _____		DISTANCE	
			TIME	
			PACE	
			HEART RATE	
			CALORIES	

Friday **8** July	☐ Ocean ☐ Pool Laps _____ Pool Length _____		DISTANCE	
			TIME	
			PACE	
			HEART RATE	
			CALORIES	

Saturday **9** July	☐ Ocean ☐ Pool Laps _____ Pool Length _____		DISTANCE	
			TIME	
			PACE	
			HEART RATE	
			CALORIES	

Sunday **10** July	☐ Ocean ☐ Pool Laps _____ Pool Length _____		DISTANCE	
			TIME	
			PACE	
			HEART RATE	
			CALORIES	

NOTES, ACHIEVEMENTS, EXTRA TRAINING

THIS WEEKS DISTANCE	
TOTAL YEARLY DISTANCE	

Monday 11 July	☐ Ocean ☐ Pool Laps _____ Pool Length _____		DISTANCE	
			TIME	
			PACE	
			HEART RATE	
			CALORIES	
Tuesday 12 July	☐ Ocean ☐ Pool Laps _____ Pool Length _____		DISTANCE	
			TIME	
			PACE	
			HEART RATE	
			CALORIES	
Wednesday 13 July	☐ Ocean ☐ Pool Laps _____ Pool Length _____		DISTANCE	
			TIME	
			PACE	
			HEART RATE	
			CALORIES	
Thursday 14 July	☐ Ocean ☐ Pool Laps _____ Pool Length _____		DISTANCE	
			TIME	
			PACE	
			HEART RATE	
			CALORIES	
Friday 15 July	☐ Ocean ☐ Pool Laps _____ Pool Length _____		DISTANCE	
			TIME	
			PACE	
			HEART RATE	
			CALORIES	
Saturday 16 July	☐ Ocean ☐ Pool Laps _____ Pool Length _____		DISTANCE	
			TIME	
			PACE	
			HEART RATE	
			CALORIES	
Sunday 17 July	☐ Ocean ☐ Pool Laps _____ Pool Length _____		DISTANCE	
			TIME	
			PACE	
			HEART RATE	
			CALORIES	

NOTES, ACHIEVEMENTS, EXTRA TRAINING

THIS WEEKS DISTANCE	
TOTAL YEARLY DISTANCE	

Monday **18** July	☐ Ocean ☐ Pool Laps _____ Pool Length _____		DISTANCE	
			TIME	
			PACE	
			HEART RATE	
			CALORIES	
Tuesday **19** July	☐ Ocean ☐ Pool Laps _____ Pool Length _____		DISTANCE	
			TIME	
			PACE	
			HEART RATE	
			CALORIES	
Wednesday **20** July	☐ Ocean ☐ Pool Laps _____ Pool Length _____		DISTANCE	
			TIME	
			PACE	
			HEART RATE	
			CALORIES	
Thursday **21** July	☐ Ocean ☐ Pool Laps _____ Pool Length _____		DISTANCE	
			TIME	
			PACE	
			HEART RATE	
			CALORIES	
Friday **22** July	☐ Ocean ☐ Pool Laps _____ Pool Length _____		DISTANCE	
			TIME	
			PACE	
			HEART RATE	
			CALORIES	
Saturday **23** July	☐ Ocean ☐ Pool Laps _____ Pool Length _____		DISTANCE	
			TIME	
			PACE	
			HEART RATE	
			CALORIES	
Sunday **24** July	☐ Ocean ☐ Pool Laps _____ Pool Length _____		DISTANCE	
			TIME	
			PACE	
			HEART RATE	
			CALORIES	

NOTES, ACHIEVEMENTS, EXTRA TRAINING

THIS WEEKS DISTANCE	
TOTAL YEARLY DISTANCE	

Monday **25** July	☐ Ocean ☐ Pool Laps _____ Pool Length _____		DISTANCE	
			TIME	
			PACE	
			HEART RATE	
			CALORIES	
Tuesday **26** July	☐ Ocean ☐ Pool Laps _____ Pool Length _____		DISTANCE	
			TIME	
			PACE	
			HEART RATE	
			CALORIES	
Wednesday **27** July	☐ Ocean ☐ Pool Laps _____ Pool Length _____		DISTANCE	
			TIME	
			PACE	
			HEART RATE	
			CALORIES	
Thursday **28** July	☐ Ocean ☐ Pool Laps _____ Pool Length _____		DISTANCE	
			TIME	
			PACE	
			HEART RATE	
			CALORIES	
Friday **29** July	☐ Ocean ☐ Pool Laps _____ Pool Length _____		DISTANCE	
			TIME	
			PACE	
			HEART RATE	
			CALORIES	
Saturday **30** July	☐ Ocean ☐ Pool Laps _____ Pool Length _____		DISTANCE	
			TIME	
			PACE	
			HEART RATE	
			CALORIES	
Sunday **31** July	☐ Ocean ☐ Pool Laps _____ Pool Length _____		DISTANCE	
			TIME	
			PACE	
			HEART RATE	
			CALORIES	

NOTES, ACHIEVEMENTS, EXTRA TRAINING

THIS WEEKS DISTANCE	
TOTAL YEARLY DISTANCE	

Monday **1** August	☐ Ocean ☐ Pool Laps _____ Pool Length _____		DISTANCE	
			TIME	
			PACE	
			HEART RATE	
			CALORIES	
Tuesday **2** August	☐ Ocean ☐ Pool Laps _____ Pool Length _____		DISTANCE	
			TIME	
			PACE	
			HEART RATE	
			CALORIES	
Wednesday **3** August	☐ Ocean ☐ Pool Laps _____ Pool Length _____		DISTANCE	
			TIME	
			PACE	
			HEART RATE	
			CALORIES	
Thursday **4** August	☐ Ocean ☐ Pool Laps _____ Pool Length _____		DISTANCE	
			TIME	
			PACE	
			HEART RATE	
			CALORIES	
Friday **5** August	☐ Ocean ☐ Pool Laps _____ Pool Length _____		DISTANCE	
			TIME	
			PACE	
			HEART RATE	
			CALORIES	
Saturday **6** August	☐ Ocean ☐ Pool Laps _____ Pool Length _____		DISTANCE	
			TIME	
			PACE	
			HEART RATE	
			CALORIES	
Sunday **7** August	☐ Ocean ☐ Pool Laps _____ Pool Length _____		DISTANCE	
			TIME	
			PACE	
			HEART RATE	
			CALORIES	

NOTES, ACHIEVEMENTS, EXTRA TRAINING

THIS WEEKS DISTANCE	
TOTAL YEARLY DISTANCE	

Monday **8** August	☐ Ocean ☐ Pool Laps _____ Pool Length _____		DISTANCE	
			TIME	
			PACE	
			HEART RATE	
			CALORIES	
Tuesday **9** August	☐ Ocean ☐ Pool Laps _____ Pool Length _____		DISTANCE	
			TIME	
			PACE	
			HEART RATE	
			CALORIES	
Wednesday **10** August	☐ Ocean ☐ Pool Laps _____ Pool Length _____		DISTANCE	
			TIME	
			PACE	
			HEART RATE	
			CALORIES	
Thursday **11** August	☐ Ocean ☐ Pool Laps _____ Pool Length _____		DISTANCE	
			TIME	
			PACE	
			HEART RATE	
			CALORIES	
Friday **12** August	☐ Ocean ☐ Pool Laps _____ Pool Length _____		DISTANCE	
			TIME	
			PACE	
			HEART RATE	
			CALORIES	
Saturday **13** August	☐ Ocean ☐ Pool Laps _____ Pool Length _____		DISTANCE	
			TIME	
			PACE	
			HEART RATE	
			CALORIES	
Sunday **14** August	☐ Ocean ☐ Pool Laps _____ Pool Length _____		DISTANCE	
			TIME	
			PACE	
			HEART RATE	
			CALORIES	

NOTES, ACHIEVEMENTS, EXTRA TRAINING

THIS WEEKS DISTANCE	
TOTAL YEARLY DISTANCE	

Monday **15** August	□ Ocean □ Pool Laps _____ Pool Length _____		DISTANCE	
			TIME	
			PACE	
			HEART RATE	
			CALORIES	

Tuesday **16** August	□ Ocean □ Pool Laps _____ Pool Length _____		DISTANCE	
			TIME	
			PACE	
			HEART RATE	
			CALORIES	

Wednesday **17** August	□ Ocean □ Pool Laps _____ Pool Length _____		DISTANCE	
			TIME	
			PACE	
			HEART RATE	
			CALORIES	

Thursday **18** August	□ Ocean □ Pool Laps _____ Pool Length _____		DISTANCE	
			TIME	
			PACE	
			HEART RATE	
			CALORIES	

Friday **19** August	□ Ocean □ Pool Laps _____ Pool Length _____		DISTANCE	
			TIME	
			PACE	
			HEART RATE	
			CALORIES	

Saturday **20** August	□ Ocean □ Pool Laps _____ Pool Length _____		DISTANCE	
			TIME	
			PACE	
			HEART RATE	
			CALORIES	

Sunday **21** August	□ Ocean □ Pool Laps _____ Pool Length _____		DISTANCE	
			TIME	
			PACE	
			HEART RATE	
			CALORIES	

NOTES, ACHIEVEMENTS, EXTRA TRAINING

THIS WEEKS DISTANCE	
TOTAL YEARLY DISTANCE	

Monday **22** August	☐ Ocean ☐ Pool Laps _____ Pool Length _____		DISTANCE TIME PACE HEART RATE CALORIES	
Tuesday **23** August	☐ Ocean ☐ Pool Laps _____ Pool Length _____		DISTANCE TIME PACE HEART RATE CALORIES	
Wednesday **24** August	☐ Ocean ☐ Pool Laps _____ Pool Length _____		DISTANCE TIME PACE HEART RATE CALORIES	
Thursday **25** August	☐ Ocean ☐ Pool Laps _____ Pool Length _____		DISTANCE TIME PACE HEART RATE CALORIES	
Friday **26** August	☐ Ocean ☐ Pool Laps _____ Pool Length _____		DISTANCE TIME PACE HEART RATE CALORIES	
Saturday **27** August	☐ Ocean ☐ Pool Laps _____ Pool Length _____		DISTANCE TIME PACE HEART RATE CALORIES	
Sunday **28** August	☐ Ocean ☐ Pool Laps _____ Pool Length _____		DISTANCE TIME PACE HEART RATE CALORIES	

NOTES, ACHIEVEMENTS, EXTRA TRAINING

THIS WEEKS DISTANCE	
TOTAL YEARLY DISTANCE	

			DISTANCE	
Monday **29** August	□ Ocean □ Pool Laps _____ Pool Length _____		TIME PACE HEART RATE CALORIES	

			DISTANCE	
Tuesday **30** August	□ Ocean □ Pool Laps _____ Pool Length _____		TIME PACE HEART RATE CALORIES	

			DISTANCE	
Wednesday **31** August	□ Ocean □ Pool Laps _____ Pool Length _____		TIME PACE HEART RATE CALORIES	

			DISTANCE	
Thursday **1** September	□ Ocean □ Pool Laps _____ Pool Length _____		TIME PACE HEART RATE CALORIES	

			DISTANCE	
Friday **2** September	□ Ocean □ Pool Laps _____ Pool Length _____		TIME PACE HEART RATE CALORIES	

			DISTANCE	
Saturday **3** September	□ Ocean □ Pool Laps _____ Pool Length _____		TIME PACE HEART RATE CALORIES	

			DISTANCE	
Sunday **4** September	□ Ocean □ Pool Laps _____ Pool Length _____		TIME PACE HEART RATE CALORIES	

NOTES, ACHIEVEMENTS, EXTRA TRAINING

THIS WEEKS DISTANCE	
TOTAL YEARLY DISTANCE	

Monday 5 September	☐ Ocean ☐ Pool Laps ———— Pool Length ————		DISTANCE	
			TIME	
			PACE	
			HEART RATE	
			CALORIES	

Tuesday 6 September	☐ Ocean ☐ Pool Laps ———— Pool Length ————		DISTANCE	
			TIME	
			PACE	
			HEART RATE	
			CALORIES	

Wednesday 7 September	☐ Ocean ☐ Pool Laps ———— Pool Length ————		DISTANCE	
			TIME	
			PACE	
			HEART RATE	
			CALORIES	

Thursday 8 September	☐ Ocean ☐ Pool Laps ———— Pool Length ————		DISTANCE	
			TIME	
			PACE	
			HEART RATE	
			CALORIES	

Friday 9 September	☐ Ocean ☐ Pool Laps ———— Pool Length ————		DISTANCE	
			TIME	
			PACE	
			HEART RATE	
			CALORIES	

Saturday 10 September	☐ Ocean ☐ Pool Laps ———— Pool Length ————		DISTANCE	
			TIME	
			PACE	
			HEART RATE	
			CALORIES	

Sunday 11 September	☐ Ocean ☐ Pool Laps ———— Pool Length ————		DISTANCE	
			TIME	
			PACE	
			HEART RATE	
			CALORIES	

NOTES, ACHIEVEMENTS, EXTRA TRAINING

THIS WEEKS DISTANCE	
TOTAL YEARLY DISTANCE	

Monday **12** September	☐ Ocean ☐ Pool Laps _____ Pool Length _____		DISTANCE	
			TIME	
			PACE	
			HEART RATE	
			CALORIES	
Tuesday **13** September	☐ Ocean ☐ Pool Laps _____ Pool Length _____		DISTANCE	
			TIME	
			PACE	
			HEART RATE	
			CALORIES	
Wednesday **14** September	☐ Ocean ☐ Pool Laps _____ Pool Length _____		DISTANCE	
			TIME	
			PACE	
			HEART RATE	
			CALORIES	
Thursday **15** September	☐ Ocean ☐ Pool Laps _____ Pool Length _____		DISTANCE	
			TIME	
			PACE	
			HEART RATE	
			CALORIES	
Friday **16** September	☐ Ocean ☐ Pool Laps _____ Pool Length _____		DISTANCE	
			TIME	
			PACE	
			HEART RATE	
			CALORIES	
Saturday **17** September	☐ Ocean ☐ Pool Laps _____ Pool Length _____		DISTANCE	
			TIME	
			PACE	
			HEART RATE	
			CALORIES	
Sunday **18** September	☐ Ocean ☐ Pool Laps _____ Pool Length _____		DISTANCE	
			TIME	
			PACE	
			HEART RATE	
			CALORIES	

NOTES, ACHIEVEMENTS, EXTRA TRAINING

THIS WEEKS DISTANCE	
TOTAL YEARLY DISTANCE	

Monday **19** September	☐ Ocean ☐ Pool Laps _____ Pool Length _____		DISTANCE	
			TIME	
			PACE	
			HEART RATE	
			CALORIES	
Tuesday **20** September	☐ Ocean ☐ Pool Laps _____ Pool Length _____		DISTANCE	
			TIME	
			PACE	
			HEART RATE	
			CALORIES	
Wednesday **21** September	☐ Ocean ☐ Pool Laps _____ Pool Length _____		DISTANCE	
			TIME	
			PACE	
			HEART RATE	
			CALORIES	
Thursday **22** September	☐ Ocean ☐ Pool Laps _____ Pool Length _____		DISTANCE	
			TIME	
			PACE	
			HEART RATE	
			CALORIES	
Friday **23** September	☐ Ocean ☐ Pool Laps _____ Pool Length _____		DISTANCE	
			TIME	
			PACE	
			HEART RATE	
			CALORIES	
Saturday **24** September	☐ Ocean ☐ Pool Laps _____ Pool Length _____		DISTANCE	
			TIME	
			PACE	
			HEART RATE	
			CALORIES	
Sunday **25** September	☐ Ocean ☐ Pool Laps _____ Pool Length _____		DISTANCE	
			TIME	
			PACE	
			HEART RATE	
			CALORIES	

NOTES, ACHIEVEMENTS, EXTRA TRAINING

| THIS WEEKS DISTANCE | |
| TOTAL YEARLY DISTANCE | |

Monday **26** September	☐ Ocean ☐ Pool Laps _____ Pool Length _____		DISTANCE	
			TIME	
			PACE	
			HEART RATE	
			CALORIES	
Tuesday **27** September	☐ Ocean ☐ Pool Laps _____ Pool Length _____		DISTANCE	
			TIME	
			PACE	
			HEART RATE	
			CALORIES	
Wednesday **28** September	☐ Ocean ☐ Pool Laps _____ Pool Length _____		DISTANCE	
			TIME	
			PACE	
			HEART RATE	
			CALORIES	
Thursday **29** September	☐ Ocean ☐ Pool Laps _____ Pool Length _____		DISTANCE	
			TIME	
			PACE	
			HEART RATE	
			CALORIES	
Friday **30** September	☐ Ocean ☐ Pool Laps _____ Pool Length _____		DISTANCE	
			TIME	
			PACE	
			HEART RATE	
			CALORIES	
Saturday **1** October	☐ Ocean ☐ Pool Laps _____ Pool Length _____		DISTANCE	
			TIME	
			PACE	
			HEART RATE	
			CALORIES	
Sunday **2** October	☐ Ocean ☐ Pool Laps _____ Pool Length _____		DISTANCE	
			TIME	
			PACE	
			HEART RATE	
			CALORIES	

NOTES, ACHIEVEMENTS, EXTRA TRAINING

THIS WEEKS DISTANCE	
TOTAL YEARLY DISTANCE	

Monday 3 October	☐ Ocean ☐ Pool Laps ——— Pool Length ———		DISTANCE	
			TIME	
			PACE	
			HEART RATE	
			CALORIES	
Tuesday 4 October	☐ Ocean ☐ Pool Laps ——— Pool Length ———		DISTANCE	
			TIME	
			PACE	
			HEART RATE	
			CALORIES	
Wednesday 5 October	☐ Ocean ☐ Pool Laps ——— Pool Length ———		DISTANCE	
			TIME	
			PACE	
			HEART RATE	
			CALORIES	
Thursday 6 October	☐ Ocean ☐ Pool Laps ——— Pool Length ———		DISTANCE	
			TIME	
			PACE	
			HEART RATE	
			CALORIES	
Friday 7 October	☐ Ocean ☐ Pool Laps ——— Pool Length ———		DISTANCE	
			TIME	
			PACE	
			HEART RATE	
			CALORIES	
Saturday 8 October	☐ Ocean ☐ Pool Laps ——— Pool Length ———		DISTANCE	
			TIME	
			PACE	
			HEART RATE	
			CALORIES	
Sunday 9 October	☐ Ocean ☐ Pool Laps ——— Pool Length ———		DISTANCE	
			TIME	
			PACE	
			HEART RATE	
			CALORIES	

NOTES, ACHIEVEMENTS, EXTRA TRAINING

THIS WEEKS DISTANCE	
TOTAL YEARLY DISTANCE	

			DISTANCE	
Monday **10** October	☐ Ocean ☐ Pool Laps ____ Pool Length ____		TIME	
			PACE	
			HEART RATE	
			CALORIES	

			DISTANCE	
Tuesday **11** October	☐ Ocean ☐ Pool Laps ____ Pool Length ____		TIME	
			PACE	
			HEART RATE	
			CALORIES	

			DISTANCE	
Wednesday **12** October	☐ Ocean ☐ Pool Laps ____ Pool Length ____		TIME	
			PACE	
			HEART RATE	
			CALORIES	

			DISTANCE	
Thursday **13** October	☐ Ocean ☐ Pool Laps ____ Pool Length ____		TIME	
			PACE	
			HEART RATE	
			CALORIES	

			DISTANCE	
Friday **14** October	☐ Ocean ☐ Pool Laps ____ Pool Length ____		TIME	
			PACE	
			HEART RATE	
			CALORIES	

			DISTANCE	
Saturday **15** October	☐ Ocean ☐ Pool Laps ____ Pool Length ____		TIME	
			PACE	
			HEART RATE	
			CALORIES	

			DISTANCE	
Sunday **16** October	☐ Ocean ☐ Pool Laps ____ Pool Length ____		TIME	
			PACE	
			HEART RATE	
			CALORIES	

NOTES, ACHIEVEMENTS, EXTRA TRAINING

THIS WEEKS DISTANCE	
TOTAL YEARLY DISTANCE	

Monday **17** October	☐ Ocean ☐ Pool		DISTANCE	
			TIME	
			PACE	
	Laps ———		HEART RATE	
	Pool Length ———		CALORIES	

Tuesday **18** October	☐ Ocean ☐ Pool		DISTANCE	
			TIME	
			PACE	
	Laps ———		HEART RATE	
	Pool Length ———		CALORIES	

Wednesday **19** October	☐ Ocean ☐ Pool		DISTANCE	
			TIME	
			PACE	
	Laps ———		HEART RATE	
	Pool Length ———		CALORIES	

Thursday **20** October	☐ Ocean ☐ Pool		DISTANCE	
			TIME	
			PACE	
	Laps ———		HEART RATE	
	Pool Length ———		CALORIES	

Friday **21** October	☐ Ocean ☐ Pool		DISTANCE	
			TIME	
			PACE	
	Laps ———		HEART RATE	
	Pool Length ———		CALORIES	

Saturday **22** October	☐ Ocean ☐ Pool		DISTANCE	
			TIME	
			PACE	
	Laps ———		HEART RATE	
	Pool Length ———		CALORIES	

Sunday **23** October	☐ Ocean ☐ Pool		DISTANCE	
			TIME	
			PACE	
	Laps ———		HEART RATE	
	Pool Length ———		CALORIES	

NOTES, ACHIEVEMENTS, EXTRA TRAINING

THIS WEEKS DISTANCE	
TOTAL YEARLY DISTANCE	

			DISTANCE	
Monday **24** October	☐ Ocean ☐ Pool		TIME	
			PACE	
	Laps _____		HEART RATE	
	Pool Length _____		CALORIES	
Tuesday **25** October	☐ Ocean ☐ Pool		DISTANCE	
			TIME	
			PACE	
	Laps _____		HEART RATE	
	Pool Length _____		CALORIES	
Wednesday **26** October	☐ Ocean ☐ Pool		DISTANCE	
			TIME	
			PACE	
	Laps _____		HEART RATE	
	Pool Length _____		CALORIES	
Thursday **27** October	☐ Ocean ☐ Pool		DISTANCE	
			TIME	
			PACE	
	Laps _____		HEART RATE	
	Pool Length _____		CALORIES	
Friday **28** October	☐ Ocean ☐ Pool		DISTANCE	
			TIME	
			PACE	
	Laps _____		HEART RATE	
	Pool Length _____		CALORIES	
Saturday **29** October	☐ Ocean ☐ Pool		DISTANCE	
			TIME	
			PACE	
	Laps _____		HEART RATE	
	Pool Length _____		CALORIES	
Sunday **30** October	☐ Ocean ☐ Pool		DISTANCE	
			TIME	
			PACE	
	Laps _____		HEART RATE	
	Pool Length _____		CALORIES	

NOTES, ACHIEVEMENTS, EXTRA TRAINING

THIS WEEKS DISTANCE	
TOTAL YEARLY DISTANCE	

Monday **31** October	☐ Ocean ☐ Pool Laps _____ Pool Length _____		DISTANCE TIME PACE HEART RATE CALORIES	
Tuesday **1** November	☐ Ocean ☐ Pool Laps _____ Pool Length _____		DISTANCE TIME PACE HEART RATE CALORIES	
Wednesday **2** November	☐ Ocean ☐ Pool Laps _____ Pool Length _____		DISTANCE TIME PACE HEART RATE CALORIES	
Thursday **3** November	☐ Ocean ☐ Pool Laps _____ Pool Length _____		DISTANCE TIME PACE HEART RATE CALORIES	
Friday **4** November	☐ Ocean ☐ Pool Laps _____ Pool Length _____		DISTANCE TIME PACE HEART RATE CALORIES	
Saturday **5** November	☐ Ocean ☐ Pool Laps _____ Pool Length _____		DISTANCE TIME PACE HEART RATE CALORIES	
Sunday **6** November	☐ Ocean ☐ Pool Laps _____ Pool Length _____		DISTANCE TIME PACE HEART RATE CALORIES	

NOTES, ACHIEVEMENTS, EXTRA TRAINING

| THIS WEEKS DISTANCE | |
| TOTAL YEARLY DISTANCE | |

Monday **7** November	☐ Ocean ☐ Pool Laps _____ Pool Length _____		DISTANCE	
			TIME	
			PACE	
			HEART RATE	
			CALORIES	

Tuesday **8** November	☐ Ocean ☐ Pool Laps _____ Pool Length _____		DISTANCE	
			TIME	
			PACE	
			HEART RATE	
			CALORIES	

Wednesday **9** November	☐ Ocean ☐ Pool Laps _____ Pool Length _____		DISTANCE	
			TIME	
			PACE	
			HEART RATE	
			CALORIES	

Thursday **10** November	☐ Ocean ☐ Pool Laps _____ Pool Length _____		DISTANCE	
			TIME	
			PACE	
			HEART RATE	
			CALORIES	

Friday **11** November	☐ Ocean ☐ Pool Laps _____ Pool Length _____		DISTANCE	
			TIME	
			PACE	
			HEART RATE	
			CALORIES	

Saturday **12** November	☐ Ocean ☐ Pool Laps _____ Pool Length _____		DISTANCE	
			TIME	
			PACE	
			HEART RATE	
			CALORIES	

Sunday **13** November	☐ Ocean ☐ Pool Laps _____ Pool Length _____		DISTANCE	
			TIME	
			PACE	
			HEART RATE	
			CALORIES	

NOTES, ACHIEVEMENTS, EXTRA TRAINING

THIS WEEKS DISTANCE	
TOTAL YEARLY DISTANCE	

Monday 14 November	☐ Ocean ☐ Pool Laps _____ Pool Length _____		DISTANCE	
			TIME	
			PACE	
			HEART RATE	
			CALORIES	
Tuesday 15 November	☐ Ocean ☐ Pool Laps _____ Pool Length _____		DISTANCE	
			TIME	
			PACE	
			HEART RATE	
			CALORIES	
Wednesday 16 November	☐ Ocean ☐ Pool Laps _____ Pool Length _____		DISTANCE	
			TIME	
			PACE	
			HEART RATE	
			CALORIES	
Thursday 17 November	☐ Ocean ☐ Pool Laps _____ Pool Length _____		DISTANCE	
			TIME	
			PACE	
			HEART RATE	
			CALORIES	
Friday 18 November	☐ Ocean ☐ Pool Laps _____ Pool Length _____		DISTANCE	
			TIME	
			PACE	
			HEART RATE	
			CALORIES	
Saturday 19 November	☐ Ocean ☐ Pool Laps _____ Pool Length _____		DISTANCE	
			TIME	
			PACE	
			HEART RATE	
			CALORIES	
Sunday 20 November	☐ Ocean ☐ Pool Laps _____ Pool Length _____		DISTANCE	
			TIME	
			PACE	
			HEART RATE	
			CALORIES	

NOTES, ACHIEVEMENTS, EXTRA TRAINING

THIS WEEKS DISTANCE	
TOTAL YEARLY DISTANCE	

Monday **21** November	☐ Ocean ☐ Pool	Laps _____ Pool Length _____	DISTANCE	
			TIME	
			PACE	
			HEART RATE	
			CALORIES	
Tuesday **22** November	☐ Ocean ☐ Pool	Laps _____ Pool Length _____	DISTANCE	
			TIME	
			PACE	
			HEART RATE	
			CALORIES	
Wednesday **23** November	☐ Ocean ☐ Pool	Laps _____ Pool Length _____	DISTANCE	
			TIME	
			PACE	
			HEART RATE	
			CALORIES	
Thursday **24** November	☐ Ocean ☐ Pool	Laps _____ Pool Length _____	DISTANCE	
			TIME	
			PACE	
			HEART RATE	
			CALORIES	
Friday **25** November	☐ Ocean ☐ Pool	Laps _____ Pool Length _____	DISTANCE	
			TIME	
			PACE	
			HEART RATE	
			CALORIES	
Saturday **26** November	☐ Ocean ☐ Pool	Laps _____ Pool Length _____	DISTANCE	
			TIME	
			PACE	
			HEART RATE	
			CALORIES	
Sunday **27** November	☐ Ocean ☐ Pool	Laps _____ Pool Length _____	DISTANCE	
			TIME	
			PACE	
			HEART RATE	
			CALORIES	

NOTES, ACHIEVEMENTS, EXTRA TRAINING

THIS WEEKS DISTANCE	
TOTAL YEARLY DISTANCE	

			DISTANCE	
Monday **28** November	☐ Ocean ☐ Pool Laps ———— Pool Length ————		TIME	
			PACE	
			HEART RATE	
			CALORIES	
Tuesday **29** November	☐ Ocean ☐ Pool Laps ———— Pool Length ————		DISTANCE	
			TIME	
			PACE	
			HEART RATE	
			CALORIES	
Wednesday **30** November	☐ Ocean ☐ Pool Laps ———— Pool Length ————		DISTANCE	
			TIME	
			PACE	
			HEART RATE	
			CALORIES	
Thursday **1** December	☐ Ocean ☐ Pool Laps ———— Pool Length ————		DISTANCE	
			TIME	
			PACE	
			HEART RATE	
			CALORIES	
Friday **2** December	☐ Ocean ☐ Pool Laps ———— Pool Length ————		DISTANCE	
			TIME	
			PACE	
			HEART RATE	
			CALORIES	
Saturday **3** December	☐ Ocean ☐ Pool Laps ———— Pool Length ————		DISTANCE	
			TIME	
			PACE	
			HEART RATE	
			CALORIES	
Sunday **4** December	☐ Ocean ☐ Pool Laps ———— Pool Length ————		DISTANCE	
			TIME	
			PACE	
			HEART RATE	
			CALORIES	

NOTES, ACHIEVEMENTS, EXTRA TRAINING

THIS WEEKS DISTANCE	
TOTAL YEARLY DISTANCE	

Monday **5** December	☐ Ocean ☐ Pool Laps _____ Pool Length _____		DISTANCE	
			TIME	
			PACE	
			HEART RATE	
			CALORIES	

Tuesday **6** December	☐ Ocean ☐ Pool Laps _____ Pool Length _____		DISTANCE	
			TIME	
			PACE	
			HEART RATE	
			CALORIES	

Wednesday **7** December	☐ Ocean ☐ Pool Laps _____ Pool Length _____		DISTANCE	
			TIME	
			PACE	
			HEART RATE	
			CALORIES	

Thursday **8** December	☐ Ocean ☐ Pool Laps _____ Pool Length _____		DISTANCE	
			TIME	
			PACE	
			HEART RATE	
			CALORIES	

Friday **9** December	☐ Ocean ☐ Pool Laps _____ Pool Length _____		DISTANCE	
			TIME	
			PACE	
			HEART RATE	
			CALORIES	

Saturday **10** December	☐ Ocean ☐ Pool Laps _____ Pool Length _____		DISTANCE	
			TIME	
			PACE	
			HEART RATE	
			CALORIES	

Sunday **11** December	☐ Ocean ☐ Pool Laps _____ Pool Length _____		DISTANCE	
			TIME	
			PACE	
			HEART RATE	
			CALORIES	

NOTES, ACHIEVEMENTS, EXTRA TRAINING

THIS WEEKS DISTANCE	
TOTAL YEARLY DISTANCE	

			DISTANCE	

Monday
12
December
- ☐ Ocean
- ☐ Pool

Laps _____
Pool Length _____

	DISTANCE	
	TIME	
	PACE	
	HEART RATE	
	CALORIES	

Tuesday
13
December
- ☐ Ocean
- ☐ Pool

Laps _____
Pool Length _____

	DISTANCE	
	TIME	
	PACE	
	HEART RATE	
	CALORIES	

Wednesday
14
December
- ☐ Ocean
- ☐ Pool

Laps _____
Pool Length _____

	DISTANCE	
	TIME	
	PACE	
	HEART RATE	
	CALORIES	

Thursday
15
December
- ☐ Ocean
- ☐ Pool

Laps _____
Pool Length _____

	DISTANCE	
	TIME	
	PACE	
	HEART RATE	
	CALORIES	

Friday
16
December
- ☐ Ocean
- ☐ Pool

Laps _____
Pool Length _____

	DISTANCE	
	TIME	
	PACE	
	HEART RATE	
	CALORIES	

Saturday
17
December
- ☐ Ocean
- ☐ Pool

Laps _____
Pool Length _____

	DISTANCE	
	TIME	
	PACE	
	HEART RATE	
	CALORIES	

Sunday
18
December
- ☐ Ocean
- ☐ Pool

Laps _____
Pool Length _____

	DISTANCE	
	TIME	
	PACE	
	HEART RATE	
	CALORIES	

NOTES, ACHIEVEMENTS, EXTRA TRAINING

THIS WEEKS DISTANCE	
TOTAL YEARLY DISTANCE	

Monday **19** December	☐ Ocean ☐ Pool Laps _____ Pool Length _____		DISTANCE	
			TIME	
			PACE	
			HEART RATE	
			CALORIES	

Tuesday **20** December	☐ Ocean ☐ Pool Laps _____ Pool Length _____		DISTANCE	
			TIME	
			PACE	
			HEART RATE	
			CALORIES	

Wednesday **21** December	☐ Ocean ☐ Pool Laps _____ Pool Length _____		DISTANCE	
			TIME	
			PACE	
			HEART RATE	
			CALORIES	

Thursday **22** December	☐ Ocean ☐ Pool Laps _____ Pool Length _____		DISTANCE	
			TIME	
			PACE	
			HEART RATE	
			CALORIES	

Friday **23** December	☐ Ocean ☐ Pool Laps _____ Pool Length _____		DISTANCE	
			TIME	
			PACE	
			HEART RATE	
			CALORIES	

Saturday **24** December	☐ Ocean ☐ Pool Laps _____ Pool Length _____		DISTANCE	
			TIME	
			PACE	
			HEART RATE	
			CALORIES	

Sunday **25** December	☐ Ocean ☐ Pool Laps _____ Pool Length _____		DISTANCE	
			TIME	
			PACE	
			HEART RATE	
			CALORIES	

NOTES, ACHIEVEMENTS, EXTRA TRAINING

THIS WEEKS DISTANCE	
TOTAL YEARLY DISTANCE	

Monday **26** December	☐ Ocean ☐ Pool Laps _____ Pool Length _____		DISTANCE	
			TIME	
			PACE	
			HEART RATE	
			CALORIES	
Tuesday **27** December	☐ Ocean ☐ Pool Laps _____ Pool Length _____		DISTANCE	
			TIME	
			PACE	
			HEART RATE	
			CALORIES	
Wednesday **28** December	☐ Ocean ☐ Pool Laps _____ Pool Length _____		DISTANCE	
			TIME	
			PACE	
			HEART RATE	
			CALORIES	
Thursday **29** December	☐ Ocean ☐ Pool Laps _____ Pool Length _____		DISTANCE	
			TIME	
			PACE	
			HEART RATE	
			CALORIES	
Friday **30** December	☐ Ocean ☐ Pool Laps _____ Pool Length _____		DISTANCE	
			TIME	
			PACE	
			HEART RATE	
			CALORIES	
Saturday **31** December	☐ Ocean ☐ Pool Laps _____ Pool Length _____		DISTANCE	
			TIME	
			PACE	
			HEART RATE	
			CALORIES	
Sunday **1** January	☐ Ocean ☐ Pool Laps _____ Pool Length _____		DISTANCE	
			TIME	
			PACE	
			HEART RATE	
			CALORIES	

NOTES, ACHIEVEMENTS, EXTRA TRAINING

THIS WEEKS DISTANCE	
TOTAL YEARLY DISTANCE	

Total Distance Swam	
Longest Swim	
Number of Swims	
Number of Races Swam	
Total Distance (Race)	
Quickest Pace (Race)	
Best Placement in a Race	
Average Race Placement	
Longest Weekly Distance	
Longest Monthly Distance	

YEARLY REFLECTION

Use this space to reflect on your year! You decide what you would like to reflect on. Some suggestion topics include:

- Proudest Moments
- Areas in which you saw improvement
- Areas to focus on for next year
- Favourite Swims
- Tips for yourself
- Favourite Races
- Everything and anything else to do with Swimming

NOTES

DATE	NOTE

DATE	NOTE

NOTES

DATE	NOTE

DATE	NOTE

NOTES

DATE	NOTE

DATE	NOTE

NOTES

DATE	NOTE

DATE	NOTE

NOTES

DATE	NOTE

DATE	NOTE

NOTES

DATE	NOTE

DATE	NOTE

NOTES

DATE	NOTE

DATE	NOTE

NOTES

DATE	NOTE

DATE	NOTE

NOTES

DATE	NOTE

DATE	NOTE

NOTES

DATE	NOTE

DATE	NOTE

NOTES

DATE	NOTE

DATE	NOTE

Thankyou for your purchase!

If you get the chance, we would love an honest review on the location in which you purchased this book. We are a small business that appreciates every review!